# REJECTION LETTERS OF FUTURE EMPLOYERS

## WITH COMMENTS

### BY MILA ILKOVA

**M**

New York

What most applicants go through.
The ones that don't are nonexistent.
It'd be hilarious if this book got a job!

1

Thank you for your interest.

We regret to advise you that after careful consideration you have not been selected for an interview on this occasion.

Despite the disappointing news, we encourage you to review other open positions.

Yours sincerely,
Team

That's fine. I was expecting a few rejections at first. Companies have their requirements, applicants have their requirements, and sometimes they just don't match each other. It's all very subjective.

Hi Mila,

We would like to thank you for your interest in the position at Company, and especially for the time you dedicated to your application. We consider ourselves very fortunate to have such qualified candidates applying for our positions.

We received a high number of applications for this position and after careful consideration, we have decided to move forward in the process with other applicants whose skills and experience more closely align with the requirements of the role.

This decision is specific to the job referenced above and does not apply to other current or future open positions. We believe your experience and education are very relevant and that's why we would like to keep in touch for future opportunities. We encourage you to contact us or apply again if you see a position that is of interest to you.

Thank you again for your interest.

Kind regards,
Talent Team

You're fucking welcome.

Hi Mila,

Thank you for your application to our company. After reviewing your work and experience, we've made the decision to not move forward at this time. I hope you don't mind if we reach out to you in the future when a position opens up that may be a good fit.
We appreciate your interest in our company and wish you success in your job search.

Best,
Recruiting Team

What if I wrote that to employers? "I hope you don't mind if I reach out to you in the future when I need to pay rent — you may be a good fit."

Dear Mila,

Thank you for your enthusiasm and interest in the position with us. We are excited about the possibility of having you on our team to help launch our dating app in a way that resonates with the local community. To move forward in the application process, we kindly ask you to undertake two important steps:

1. **Experience**: Please download our app and create your account. We believe that a deep understanding of the app is essential for crafting an event that truly represents our brand. Spend some time exploring the features and getting to know what makes us unique.

2. **Share Your Vision**: Could you please email us a brief proposal, no more than 2-3 sentences, outlining your concept for a launch party tailored to your city? Consider strategies that would effectively attract new users and introduce them to us, keeping local preferences and culture in mind.

Your insights and creativity are valuable to us, and we look forward to seeing your vision for bringing our app to life in your community.

Warm regards,

Mecs

Of course, my creativity and insights are valuable. That's exactly why it's called a job: skills in exchange for $$$.

Hello Mila,

We're excited to move you forward to the next stage!

As the **next step** in your application process, we are gathering some insights — your input helps us understand you better. You will **receive a separate email** from our partner platform with instructions to **submit a short recording** answering a couple of questions related to your culture. Please submit your recording at your earliest convenience. It will be reviewed in a timely manner but please be patient as we do have a large number of applicants.

Best Regards,

The Team

Please record a short film about your skills, submit it to 7 world-known film festivals, and if the jury puts you on the shortlist only then submit it to this job at your earliest convenience. We are a multi-diverse company, so please make sure you tango in a sombrero while opera-singing in Portuguese. We look forward to it.

Dear Mila,

Thank you for taking the time to submit your application (Remote or Hybrid) position. We are glad that you are interested in a career with us and we're here to help you find your perfect fit.
We encourage you to visit our Career Center frequently and continue to look for opportunities that match your interests.

Thank you,
Talent Acquisition Team.

Note: You must use the same email you used to log in to the career center when applying for jobs.

Currently, on a research/walk/ eat/sleep routine, but I can make time for your company.

Dear Mila,

Thank you for your interest. We receive many strong applications for our job openings. After reviewing your CV, we are unable to move forward with your candidacy at this time, but we encourage you to please apply again in the future.

We wish you the best of luck in your search and will keep you in mind for future opportunities.

If you have any questions, please don't hesitate to email us.

Best,
Talent Acquisition Team

Yeah, I have a question. Why don't companies let you choose your own pronouns? I am obviously a woman, no need to clarify that, but after 3 glasses of wine, I identify as Empress.

8

Hi Mila,

Thank you for your application for the position at the Foundation.

We have had an overwhelming amount of applications for this position, and therefore our screening process is taking a lot longer than normal. Please know that your application is still pending review and we will be in touch soon. Apologies for this inconvenience.

Talk soon,
Director of Recruiting

Is this application going to take over 9 years as well, just like the immigration process in this country?

# 9

Job market is terrible.

I am sorry. I have let you down — big time.

Paul.

Oh, Paul. Maybe RECRUITING is NOT YOUR CUP of tea. Join me in the job SEARCH — you need it, too.

# 10

    Thank you for your interest in the position. We will review your materials and will get back to you if we wish to pursue your candidacy.

I spent my whole life developing an actual personality, and now an algorithm decides whether I used enough of keywords to be selected? This is bullshit.

# 11

Dear Mila,

We are currently reviewing your application. If your profile is a good fit for this position, we will contact you about next steps. We may also consider your application for other positions. This could happen a few times and it is part of our recruitment process.

Is your profile telling your story?

A key part of our review process is to assess your Candidate Profile with job requirements. Please ensure your profile is accurate and extensive as it is our first step in getting to know you. You can build your profile by importing information from your resume or manually updating it. To view your application updates, click My Applications.

All companies should subscribe to my Candidate Profile for $10 a month, so while I wait for their robots to highlight their favorite keywords in my resume, I can make a living off of the subscription. And for an extra $20 a month, tailored only to my fan companies, I will send personalized cover letters, pervertedly lying about how I'd love to work for them.

Hi Mila,

Thank you for your interest in the role.

   Unfortunately, at this time we have decided to go in another direction. We will be hiring for additional positions in December/January, so please stay in touch.

   Thank you

Which direction is it? Maybe I need to go there as well. Perhaps that's the route I should take instead of this horse track I run at in circles over and over, where no one bids on me winning.

Hi Mila,

Thanks for getting in touch. We don't have
the need at the moment.

Best of luck

You can have my need — I've
got plenty and can share lots
of needs. Sharing is caring.

Dear Mila,

Thank you for your email and for sharing your resume with us. We do not currently have any openings.

If you are interested in employment opportunities with us, please send your resume to the Human Resources Department.

Recruitment Unit

Happiness loves silence. I haven't received any texts or calls in 2 days. People are trying so hard to make me happy.

Dear Applicant,

Thank you for submitting your application. This email is to acknowledge our receipt of your application. We will review your application and will be back in touch with the next steps.

Your Reference number is: VSMS2330

Sincerely,
Team

-- do not reply --

Okay, this is not going the way I thought it would. But life goes on, and there's a lot to do and see in New York City.

Hi,

We're glad you're here. We'll keep you in the loop with our latest news and special offers.

Explore more of New York City and enjoy 10% off your next experience with promo code **"WELCOME716"**

Get more when you book directly with us.

Sincerely Yours
Recruitment Team

Did I apply to a job OR subscribe to their promotional emails?

While we won't be proceeding with your application at this time, your qualifications were impressive, and we encourage you to continue pursuing opportunities that align with your career goals.

I like good boots. After I already made the purchase, Instagram kept advertising me the boots I already owned. My friend and I spoke about traveling — Instagram showed me tourist stuff in NYC, pretending it doesn't know where I live. I am single — Instagram keeps showing me ads with wedding dresses. It's either a way to annoy me or the Insta fortune cookie knows something I don't know yet. Okay, Insta, get synced with Tinder and Amazon and get me the delivery. And, fine, add the wedding dress you advertised — it looked nice.

Good afternoon!

You have received this email because you applied to be considered for a job position. To proceed with your application, you need to complete the corporate business simulation "Business Cats."

The business simulation will assess your analytical and communication skills. You need to reach "Level 1." To do this, you must complete the training and play two games with bots.

After successfully completing "Business Cats," you need to send a screenshot of your result and your updated resume to this email. The deadline to complete this task is 3 days from the date of this message.

If you have any questions, we will be happy to answer them.

I made that mistake before and will never do it again. No, I will not do your stupid assignment — I don't do homework. 2 Master's degrees, 4 languages, 8 books, 18 years of experience, and a 190-page portfolio is enough. Analyze better.

Dear Mila,

I'm sorry I didn't see your email when it first landed and want you to know how seriously we consider each email we receive. I am sorry to say, though, that unfortunately I do not have good news as we have moved forward with the application process and you have not been selected.

Please know I wish you all the best.

Please know I wish you all the so-so because all the bad would be way too good for you.

Dear Applicant,

We regret to inform you that we have reviewed your application and were unable to verify your eligibility for the position due to the following reason(s):

The employee (applicant) cannot complete the submission information: Cover letter.

If you have questions please feel free to contact us.

Best,
Hiring Team

Shower thought number 18344:
The last thing you want to see on stage is a drummer singing.

# 21

We are so grateful for your interest. We had an overwhelming response and were humbled by the exceptional caliber of candidates who applied. Please be assured that your application was given full consideration. Unfortunately, we have chosen another candidate.

Which one is it: fortunately or un-fortunately? Unfortunately... Eh...
I saw a homeless person lying in the street under the sign "NO STANDING Anytime." Unbelievably law-obedient citizen: he peed all over himself but still obeyed the rules.

Good morning Mila,

Thank you for your interest in the open role.

We will review your resume and contact you, if you are selected to move forward in the process.

Kind regards,
Human Resources Generalist

Went to the Metropolitan Opera. Everything's great in American ballet theater: the orchestra with unique music, the stage decorations, the costumes, the story development, and the dramatic dying of all characters. One thing is missing: actual ballet dancing instead of dramatic walking on stage in pointe shoes.

Dear Mila,

Thank you very much for letting us consider you, but I'm afraid we're going to pass. We wish you all the best in finding an opportunity elsewhere.

Best wishes,
Talent Management

------------------

Shower thought number 19100: Social clubs for rich people only — kind of a pointless idea. It's the majority of people who know real life and can share various aspects of it.

Thank you for your email. I am out of office and will only be checking emails sporadically.

Should this require immediate attention, please call (860) 536-3795.

Thank you!

Every place in New York is now "hidden" and "secret," but in reality packed with tourists. For God's sake, can you all please stop with the "hidden" and "secret" places in New York and route all tourists back to Times Square and Broadway, like in the old days? Thanks.

Dear Mila,

We are pleased to inform you that your application has been received and you do not need to do anything further at this stage. We have attached the Terms and Conditions, which we advise you to read again carefully.

We take great care in evaluating every application we receive. Before we accept or reject an applicant, we always carry out specific research, which can require the expertise of external consultants.

We will aim to process your application within 12 weeks. Once we have reviewed your application, we will contact you with our decision.

Kind regards,
Management Team

The only reason I'll wait in line is if the place is selling time and can make me 25 again.

Hello! This email is not actively monitored.

***This email may be confidential. If you are not the intended recipient, please notify us immediately and delete this copy from your system. Nothing in this email creates a contract for a transaction, and the sender does not have authority to bind a party to a contract via written or verbal communication. We have taken precautions to minimize the risk of transmitting software viruses, but we advise you to carry out your own virus checks on any attachment to this message. We cannot accept liability for any loss or damage caused by software viruses. Though information is believed to be correct, it is presented subject to errors, omissions, changes or withdrawal without notice.

What if a crazy person screaming in the city is the only one who knows the essence of being while all others are brainwashed?

If your application is successful, we will notify you by email to let you know that your profile has been shortlisted.

Please note that only a small number of applicants meeting all our criteria are accepted for an interview.

Thank you for contacting us.

I don't overuse specific words so their meaning evokes maximum feelings. I also use exclamation points far less than I say "I love you" or "I miss you." If you see me use an exclamation point — something truly outstanding happened. Or something annoyed me, outstandingly.

I will follow up next Monday. Give me a few days to digest it. It won't be read by a machine but by a human!!!

Senior Major Account Manager

Okay, human!!! I'll wait!!!

Senior Major Manager Worldwide Director General President of Global Teams and Universal Transatlantic Corporations, Associates and Sons.

Thank you for your interest in joining our team. While we review your application and other materials, we request that you follow us on social media.

09:44 pm
Instead of dressing up to go out to dance I just had carrots with hummus for dinner and plan on going to sleep soon. Rehearsing I have a job I have to wake up for.

Hi, Mila. Unfortunately, I don't think you are a good match for this position. Good luck with your job search. And thank you for your time.

Oh, right, I should check my matches on Tinder.

"Hey, Mila. What's up!"

"Hey. I just ate such a juicy apple, it's all over my hands up to elbows."

"That sounds sticky. Sticky is like my worst nightmare. I basically use a wet wipe between every Buffalo wing. How did you even type that with your sticky-sticky hands?"

"I typed with my sticky-sticky elbows. I'm assuming fingering is your worst nightmare as well?"

Houston, I think we have a problem. The sticky guy didn't stick to us.

Hello,
Thanks for your email.

I am currently unavailable. Please contact someone else for assistance.

I am attractive, intelligent, caring, and creative — I am so overqualified to be dealing with this.

Hello, Mila — thank you for contacting us.

Besides submitting your resume by email and on the job board website all applications must be submitted on our careers site, too. It is required and non-negotiable.
Only resumes submitted 3 times will be considered. Thank you for understanding.

VP, HR OPERATIONS & COMPLIANCE

I am so overly—exhausted to be dealing with this.

Hi there!

Email received. I'll take a look and get back to you next week.

Have a nice weekend!

There should be an app for all overqualified candidates so they can finally find a job, I mean we can, I mean I can, finally.

Laziness attacked me and took hostage. No job applications today.

## 35

And today.

Dear Mila,

Thank you for your interest.

Could you please fill out a Candidate Profile and resubmit it? We cannot accept applications with CVs only.

At the moment we do not have any vacancies, but we keep profiles on file.

If you are interested in future vacancies, feel free to send a CV once again, and we will keep your profile for future openings. If you prefer not to send it now but are still interested, you can keep an eye out for future advertisements. As we recruit several times a year, we keep an open recruitment process...

Read on the News app:
"What BCC Is, and Why You're a Terrible Person If You Don't Use It. You don't need to wait even a single day to enjoy a completely different email experience."

Ew, perverts. Who the hell "enjoys" emails?

Hi Mila,

Thanks for submitting your resume. We would like to set up an in person interview on Tuesday or Wednesday next week.

As a reminder, this is a job that requires you to work at least three days a week in person at the Theater Center in Times Square. The other two days can be in person or remotely. The job pays $25/hour or $1000/week for a 40-hour week. You would be eligible for insurance benefits after six months.

We want to hire someone with enough of a background in the industry to measure analytics as well as create initiatives.

None of this is negotiable so if you are not currently in New York or don't feel comfortable with the salary, please don't move forward with the interview. We don't want to waste your time — or ours!

But if you are interested in this job we would love to meet with you! So if interested and available, please email back with your preferred time either on Tuesday from 1-3 or on Wednesday from 10-1.

Best,
Cathy

Cathy, for $25/hour you can measure analytics and create initiatives yourself.

Dear Mila,

Thank you very much for your information.
It would be great to meet in a short Zoom call to discuss networking.

Networking?
Did I miss all the offensive words of the year again?
Did someone feel offended by the word "WORK" so now it's called "networking"? How did they rename "networking"? "Drinking with mostly unpleasant strangers?"

Dear Mila,

The vacancy has been out for a bit and we are
finalizing a recruitment process at the moment.

Best,
Dani

Marshal, my dearest cat,

It is time for you to step in.
I am not asking you to share our
expenses — I am asking you to be
the man of our household and take
care of us. It is your turn. Besides,
people think your face is cuter than
mine. On my hand, I promise to play
with you all the time, which I already
do anyway.

Dear Applicant,

Thanks so much for letting us take a look at your resume and please forgive us for responding with a form letter. The volume of submissions we receive, however, makes it impossible to correspond with everyone personally.

Unfortunately, we have chosen another candidate at this time. We wish you the best of luck in finding another opportunity and we thank you, once again, for letting us consider your resume.

If you think it's unfortunate that you have chosen another candidate, then why have you chosen another candidate?

Thank you for applying, but after flipping a coin, we've decided to go in another direction. Best of luck with your future job!

*****Please address any questions regarding our responses to the email address of the Hiring Manager by consulting the staff page of our website.*****

What do I want in life?
An independent woman answer: start a business.
An honest answer: a waterfront house, kids, and a husband to take care of everything. You can have my vote back — the election process doesn't require it anyway.

Thanks, Mila.

I hope your man is this quick
with you in bed.
I hope this is how long your
freshly colored hair roots last.
I hope this is how long you feel
joy in life.
You're welcome.

Thank you for giving us the chance to consider your resume. While your experience is impressive and outstanding, we decided to hire someone whose experience fits better.

Ma has me saved in her phone as America. The first letter A is easy to search in contacts — I am her first one. My cousin is saved in her phone as Avtobus — same principle. And Ma sometimes mistakenly calls me my dad's name, because she is so used to it and my dad's name is the one she says the most daily. I can never run out of inspiration with my Ma, but I am running out of patience with this job search. Kind of ironic because I hate running.

Dear Ms. Mila,

Thank you so much for your email. Unfortunately, however, we have decided to move forward with other candidates. We encourage you to continue to apply elsewhere, and we wish you every success in your career. Thanks again for thinking of us.

If you do not know where you are going, any road will take you there, they say. Why am I still on the road and not there yet?

Thank you for your interest in the position and for taking the time to apply. After careful consideration, we regret to inform you that we have decided to move forward with other candidates whose qualifications more closely align with our current needs.

I need a digital version of me who will be busy sending emails and work applications to all these companies while the real me does what she loves the most: writing books.

Hi Mila,

Thanks for this. We're a small agency, and very selective, and your resume didn't seem quite right for us.

Best of luck.

Brighton beach these days is more Odessa than Odessa.

# 47

Thank you for applying, but after consulting a Magic Ball, we've decided to go in another direction.

Where do they all go when they decide to go? All RECRUiTERS aNd hiRiNg maNagERS aNd HR should go to theiR owN customiZed hell wheRe the devil makes them wRite coveR letteRS aNd theN REjects them, wRite, REject, wRite, REject, REpeat, REpeat, REpeat, REpeat, foR eteRNity.

Mila, I am so sorry not to offer you the position at this time.

"Wherever we go, we must go naked and alone," Henry Miller wrote. When I apply for jobs, I am alone and, more often than not, naked. Nudity doesn't sell as well anymore, I guess.

## 49

Thank you for applying, but after consulting our taro guru, we've decided to go in another direction.

The area near the Plaza Hotel smells like a mix of Chanel and horseshit — the famous diversity of New York City.

Thank you for your application! We decided to put the vacancy on hold.

I wish you luck on your journey!

A friend of mine knows how to say "I'm tired" in 50 languages.
I know 50 facial expressions to show frustration.

We are only reviewing resumes on a referral basis. Please refer to our website for details.

You network, someone else networks, and when you both share your networks, the possibilities expand significantly. Instead, it feels like everyone is guarding their contacts like sensitive CIA documents. Stinginess means hoarding connections like they're rare collectibles. Favors are meant to be returned; otherwise, they become commodities.

THIS IS AN AUTO REPLY. Thank you for your interest. We have received your e-mail and your resume will be reviewed shortly.

NOTE: Please do not send e-mails unless specifically requested by us.

****THIS IS AN AUTO REPLY****

Friend: Feel free to commit any crime you want. I'll bail you out of jail.
Mila: Nah, I'm over him.

While your qualifications were impressive, we have decided to pursue a candidate who fits our vision of "ideal" a bit more closely — specifically, someone who possesses the ability to mind-read office plants.

This year, I really want to have fun, fall in love, and have some luck. C'mon, Santa, you lazy fatfuck, get to work!

Dear Mila,

After much consideration, I'll be regretfully
stepping aside.

Wishing you the very best of luck. I wish I
had the time to respond in a personal manner.

Life is good, though after 10
years in NYC, I suddenly heard all
the noise and saw all the trash
in the streets, and I hate it.

Ah, the bittersweet symphony of job applications...

Congratulations on making it to the final round of Who Wants to Work Here.

You have not been selected.

Sincerely,
Hiring Team

They all are so sincere in telling me to go fuck myself...

Re: Automatic reply

Hello!

I am away from my desk until further notice and I look forward to being in touch when I return.

Thanks.

If we choose each other, we could be tired together, not pay attention to others together, finish projects together. Wait a minute. Is it just me or this is perfect for both LinkedIn and Tinder?

For a writer, you didn't seem to have much to say in your cover letter.

If you're uninterested then I wish you the best.

Why do companies expect me to write a fan-fiction letter about them? They see my resume for the first time, I see the company name for the first time — we are in the same boat in this blind process.

Hi Mila,
All the best.

A pit bull needs lots of RUNNING and playing and discipline. So does a man. It would be fun to give a super cute nickname, like "Bubbles," to a pit bull, OR a massive man.

Thank you for your email.

If your request is administrative, it will be answered promptly.

If you have submitted a resume, we appreciate your patience. As we receive many applications, we cannot send personal rejection letters.

What if my resume is not right?
I will redo it in 8 different versions
of keywords so the scanning AI
will have a multiple orgasm from my
perfect SEO.

You are receiving this message as confirmation that your resume was received.
Do not reply to this email. Please include your portfolio as a reply in your original email thread.

While we endeavor to respond to every email, due to the volume of applications we receive, it may not always be possible.

If we decide to pursue your candidacy, we will be in touch with you. We appreciate your understanding.

\*\*Please do not respond to this email unless requested.\*\*

Under no circumstances should you attempt to contact us. Send us an email but don't try to talk to us. We will not attempt to respond either, we promise. As a family-operated business since the early 20th century, we always stand by our promises.

Thank you for your application. We respect the time and effort that you put into the process, and this is a courtesy auto-response to acknowledge receipt of your resume.

Thank you, and we look forward to considering you!

The plan with 8 different versions of my resume did not help.

## 62

Interviews, Zoom, blah blah blah. Even though you already sent us your resume, please repeat it multiple times because we paid zero atten- tion to it, but you should know our company's story better than your family's.

Why are they all asking where I see myself in 5 years and not whether I am happy now?

Position has been closed.

Cordially,

Joe.

I am starting to feel like I'm
trying too hard to work with
people who believe Earth is flat.

Your resume has been received.

Your application is important to us.

Please know that every application is given extensive consideration. Bear in mind that oftentimes we might interview multiple candidates before a decision is reached.

In all of your endeavors, we wish you the best, and we thank you for the privilege to review your application.

Many thanks.

How bad is the market, really?
So bad that even pimps make
their whores do free internships
first, or is the economy still
okay-ish?

Thank you for applying.

Please don't take a pass as a comment on you or your skills; it isn't intended to be one.

We wish you the best of luck.

*Please do not respond as this is an automated response.

Some people possibly entered their early midlife crisis. It seems like everyone is either doing drugs or buying a bicycle these days (as if I were involuntarily rolling in bicycler gang circles). Nobody buys a red convertible anymore because nobody can afford it.

Dear Mila,

   Thank you very much for applying to us and we
are sorry to say we don't feel that we can offer you the position.

*Okay, Google, look up top-
notch activities in any
season besides sleep.*

# 67

Thank you for your email. I am away from my desk. Thank you for your patience and understanding.

On an international level, a week full of news is never a good thing.

Hi!

After many fruitful years I've decided to leave. If you want to reach me to hear about my new work as a psychedelic guide, you can email me back. Otherwise, please don't.

What's a psychedelic guide? You know all the drug spots in the city, literally? The tourism industry has changed a lot, but not in a good way.

Thanks so much!

*CONFIDENTIALITY NOTICE: This e-mail and any attachments, including photographs, are confidential and may be protected by legal privilege. If you are not the intended recipient, be aware that any disclosure, copying, distribution or use of this e-mail or any attachment is prohibited. If you have received this e-mail in error, please notify us immediately by returning it to the sender and delete this copy from your system. Thank you.*

*CONFIDENTIALITY NOTICE: The book or any portion of it, as well as the author's personal data, including but not limited to search engine history, online orders, and occasional nudes, can be purchased directly from the author. Readers can send their data, including but not limited to penis pictures and cat and dog videos — all are equally valuable.

*Privacy Policy for pictures and videos does not exist. All data will be used at the discretion of the author.

Thanks, but you do not sound right for our small agency.
Please keep this email for your records.

Wrote 2 jokes:

"He's an atheist. Every time he comes home, he fills himself with food until he is full because Jesus doesn't fulfill him."

"For a while, he did not love himself, possibly because he was Catholic and the only person he was supposed to love was Jesus."

And the world will never know because book agents rejected my books.

Dear Mila Ilkova,

Thank you for sending us the details of your proposed record attempt for "Most Rejected Author by Book Agents." Unfortunately, after thoroughly reviewing your application with members of our research team, we regret to inform you that we cannot accept your proposal as a Guinness World Records title.

Our team of expert Records Managers receives thousands of new record proposals every year from all over the world. Each of these proposals is carefully assessed to determine whether they meet a stringent set of criteria. Every record verified by Guinness World Records must reflect a level of existing competition in a particular field, be measurable by a single superlative, be verifiable, standardizable, breakable, and clearly present an element of skill.

Once again, thank you for contacting Guinness World Records.

Kind regards,
Records Management Team

I applied to Guinness World Records as the most rejected author and got rejected. This is hilarious.

Thank you for applying. This is an auto-reply to acknowledge receipt of your message. Due to the high number of applications, we are unfortunately unable to respond to each.

Thank you and best wishes.

A job opening for a forensic accountant. What do they calculate? Maximum credit lines for corpses?

Wish you all the best


Sent from my iPhone


How cool would it be to make my
name a hashtag and make it
marketable? So, I checked it.
MI. Abbreviation for Major Issue,
Myocardial Infraction, Michigan,
Minority Institutions, Mortgage
Insurance, Mental Illness, More
Info, Miscellaneous Item. Score!

Добрый день!

Вы заполнили форму "Как попасть?" на нашем сайте в разделе "Карьера", а так же для лучшей обратной связи прошли небольшой опрос, который помог нам познакомиться поближе.

HR-специалисты нашей компании внимательно ознакомились с Вашей кандидатурой и решили, что на данном этапе мы не готовы сделать вам предложение о работе.

Подписывайся на обновления в соц сетях, а также узнавай всю актуальную информацию о жизни компании, чтобы не пропустить интересную вакансию.

They started rejecting me
in Russian. Enchanté, блядь,
pardon my French.

Thank you for the interest you've expressed in The Company & Such. We assure you that every resume we receive is read and evaluated. If you don't hear from us within 30 days after you sent your email, please know that we have considered your candidacy but determined that it would not be a good fit for us.

----

The Company & Such Staff

Things don't have to be cool or fun all the time. Regular is fine too. I like regular — it makes cool things cooler.

Automatic reply: I am off duty until Tuesday.

Everything is about wording.
Going to a private wine tasting
at your friend's house means you'll
be sitting on the couch watching
TV while getting drunk. Excellent
verbal communication skills mean
"buttlicking" – a standard skill for
both resumes and dating. Being a
content creator means you're
posting selfies. No matter how
fancy the wording is, the essence
stays the same.

## 11

Thank you for your interest in the agency.
We are closed to new job openings and do not accept applications until further notice.

Then why post new job openings if you are closed to new job openings?
This is nonsense.
Let's make love and borsch.
Also, who decided to spell borsch with T at the end? There's no T at the end!
It's offensive that someone who doesn't speak the language tells me how to spell it. There! I got offended. I'm in trend.

## 18

Hi Mila,

I received feedback from the supervisor. Unfortunately, we cannot offer you cooperation due to a significant time difference.

We wish you success in your future job search and career development. We are confident that you will find an excellent opportunity that matches your skills and ambitions.

What's a USAF veteran? United States As Fuck veteran? Oh, it's Air Force As Fuck. AFAF — the sound of a dog sneezing. I gotta go for a walk or something...

## 19

I have a girlfriend of 9 months and she just moved in fuck off whore.

Huh? I mean... congratulations and all, but... huh? The written communication style of this future employer requires adjustment.

Hello,
No thanks.
All best.

Water always flushes away the unnecessary and is a harbinger of good. I went on a trip to Niagara Falls; I had to, because the amount of shit I put myself through could only be washed away by that much water. The gimmick helps — the cleanse is wonderful.

"It's either the American Dream or American Falls," the tour guide jokes, referring to the yearly number of attempted suicides.

No one has survived the American Falls; a few who tried to kill themselves have survived the fast flow of the Niagara River. Well, some people can't do anything right.

# 81

Thank you so much for applying. We were especially impressed by your resume, but we regret to inform you that we had to go with someone else. While we won't be moving forward with your application, we'd love to keep in touch in case our chosen candidate wins the lottery and decides to move to the south of Italy to publicly ruin wooden furniture with green paint on Instagram.

At Niagara Falls, I stay for the evening fireworks. A woman next to me, amazed by the colors and frequency, exclaims, "So beautiful! So much pollution!" which makes me laugh hysterically.

Hi Mila,

Thanks.
At first sight I don't think it's a good fit
for us.

Best,
DF

Hi Dickfuck,
Well, big deal, take a second sight
and third sight and as many
sights as you need until it's a good
fit. Take your time, but not too long.
I'm patient — not that I've been
waiting since Yugoslavia ceased
to exist, but I do have my limits.

Dear Mila,

Thank you for taking the time to fill in our application form.

This has been sent to our database and will be read by me or someone in our recruitment team. As soon as we move forward, we will contact you by e-mail or telephone (we will not contact you until we move forward).

If we are satisfied with your qualifications and experience, you will have a telephone interview and if you fulfill our requirements, we will then discuss rates, send you our contract and assign you some tasks and ...off we go!

Meanwhile, check us out and like us on Facebook and have a look at our Reviews which might be of interest to you.

Kind Regards
Head of Trainer Recruitment

Fun plan for the night: buy wine and annoy myself with overthinking.
Eh, Macarena. Ay.

Hi Mila,

Thank you so much for your application. The Struggles & Struggles is grateful for your interest in this opportunity.

The Struggles & Struggles team will be connecting back with those applicants whose experiences align most closely with the needs of the Struggles & Struggles.

If you have any questions in the meantime, please don't hesitate to reach out to me.

Best,
Associate, Social Impact and CEO & Board Practices

Hey, Struggles and Struggles, I struggle too. Let's combine our struggles, find more people who struggle, and expand to Struggles, Struggles and Struggles and Associates.

# 85

Thanks for writing!

My email has changed. I am no longer with the company.

--
If you are a resident of the European Economic Area, you have additional rights with regard to the way we hold and process your personal data — to find out more, please see our Privacy Policy.

Can we find love in a hopeless place?
We don't have another planet so...
Realistic response but optimistic.
Can we find a job on this planet,
for god's sake?!

Hi Mila,

We should know more in the next several weeks. I will be sure to be back in touch as soon as we do.

Turn any opportunity you have into something memorable, they say. Thus, the book number 9. Enjoy.

Thanks Mila

Nice work!

I'm not in the market for a new hire. I'm happy being the way things are. But if I decide on a change I shall call you.

All best

Sent from my iPhone

Someone told me that I don't look like a writer because I have a clean haircut, and his assumption is that all writers have Einstein-style haircuts. Well, I also don't look like I need a thick paycheck to rely on, and yet here we are.

# 88

We have received your inquiry. Due to increased volume as a result of social media activity, the response time to your inquiry has increased to approximately 20 business days.

Phew, good. I don't feel like working today anyway.

Your resume has been received.

And I will never know what happened to it. Did you see it? Did you read it? Did you consider it? Was it received by the Black-Hole Universe? Did Boing mess up again, so no response is coming back to Earth?

Discover Technology Career Opportunities

Looking for your next role? As we continue to witness rapid advancements in the technology industry, the demand for skilled professionals remains high. This presents an opportune time for you to explore and seize new career opportunities.

We cover a number of sectors within the technology industry.

Submit your updated resume, and when one of our talent experts finds a role that suits you, they will be in touch. Alternatively, explore a wide range of roles at the click of a button.

Why does it feel like America is against me? I personally don't have any natural resources to start building democracy out of me.

# 91

Dear Mila,

Thank you for the opportunity to consider, your experience and skills. We have decided to move forward with another candidate.

Best of luck in finding the perfect work.

Oh, a job opening for a data scientist! They better find one quickly to apply all those data models so science can answer one important question: how did we end up in a world this fucked up? Does science agree? Did the data models get offended again? Okay, never mind. Where's my imaginary rifle?

We are writing to inform you that after a rigorous recruitment process, we have filled the position.

Again, we are so appreciative of your application and hope you will consider exploring other opportunities with us. In the meantime, please accept our warmest wishes for your future endeavors.

Hey, FBI, I was only joking about a rifle. I don't even have one. I don't even want one. I can't even afford the imaginary one. But if you see my FBI guy lover, tell him I miss him.

Dear Sir/Madam Ilkova,

We are pleased to confirm receipt of your application for the Job Opening 238125.

Your application will be given due consideration along with all other applications. You will be kept informed of the status of your application throughout the process. You may follow the status of your application in your account under "Careers Home" / "My Applications". Should you move forward in the process, you may be contacted for further assessment. You will also be notified once the recruitment process is completed.

Further information, including an Instructional Manual for the Applicant, is available in the Application Process section of the Careers Portal, or by clicking the "Manuals" link at the top right corner of your homepage when you are logged in.

Please do not respond to this system-generated e-mail. You can reach us through the "Contact us" feature on the top right corner of the website.

Thank you for your interest in this position.

Yours sincerely,

Office of Human Resources Management

*Eat, pray, love.*
*Wait, wait, wait...wait again*
*until nothing matters anymore.*

Thank you for your interest in employment with our Hosted Agency Partners. Please note, your submittal has been received and is being reviewed by the appropriate party. If your message merits a response, one of our representatives will contact you shortly.

Please verify your message contains the necessary information, including the Job Title, Agency, Job Number, and — if applicable — your Resume/Cover Letter. Failure to include the required information may result in delays and/or your resume not being considered for the specified position(s).

Due to the size of the applicant pool, you will be contacted if you are selected for an interview or if we require further information from you. Our Human Resources department is unable to provide status updates during the hiring process.

Instead of swiping on Tinder, I have to go network and meet new people to possibly avoid sending out resumes. In a simple online search for where to meet people, all results show various dating apps, including Tinder. That's it — just tell me who to sleep with.

Thank you for your interest. Upon review, un-fortunately, we will not be making an offer. You have our most sincere condolences on the path to your career success.

"Hey. I just wanted to wish you a happy birthday tomorrow and I didn't want to bother you on your birthday. I hope you are doing ok. I think of you often and I'm always wondering how you are doing. I hope you are well. Please contact me if you'd ever like to. I live alone upstate in a big house with my dog for about six months now. It's great here. If you are unattached I hope you accept an invitation to visit one day. I really do think of you."

An email from my ex. Like I want to deal with this now... or ever again. Thank you for your interest, but I have decide to go with another candidate.

Thank you for your CV.
If there is a vacancy suitable for your professional skills, we will contact you.

An American girl had to get a medical
exam to finish her work permit application in France. She arrived at the
doctor's office for a routine checkup,
undressed, and the exam was conducted while she was entirely naked.
She was expecting a gown, the doctor, confused, was respectful of the
different cultural approach. The room
was filled with an overall awkward-
ness, but it wasn't too ohmygodable;
both were adults, after all. There's
no such thing as gowns in Europe for
a regular medical exam. I bet that
stupid bitch has a well-paying job
and at least 10 people depend on her
decisions.

**From:** bqczn-6674204776@job.craigslist.org
**Date:** Tuesday, August 21, 2018 1:29 PM
**To:** c5cb8015531b35aaa93b6de77f5495f5@reply.craigslist.org
**Subject:** Re: Assistant to A-list Hollywood Screenwriter/Director

Dear Mila,

Thank you for your interest in the position. A couple questions. Are you perfectly fluent in French, and, if so, how did you acquire it? Why would you want this position? Finally, do you have a cv you can send to me? The position involves self-publishing and marketing my most recent novel, helping to edit a screenplay I'm writing for Tom Hanks, editing a book on caretaking for a cancer patient which I'm completing, and, of most importance, helping me with the research and structure for a play I'm writing on François Premier which will be in both French and English, first opening in Paris with Roman Polanski directing, then in New York, and finally as a screenplay. Most of the research material will be in French. It's a full-time position.

Best wishes,
Jeremy Leven

**From:** c5cb8015531b35aaa93b6de77f5495f5@reply.
craigslist.org
**Sent:** Tuesday, August 21, 2018 2:25 PM
**To:** bqczn-6674204776@job.craigslist.org
**Subject:** Re: Assistant to A-list Hollywood
Screenwriter/Director


Dear Jeremy,

I did my Master's in Lyon, France, so yes, I
speak French. To be completely honest with you,
I haven't practiced it for some time; however,
it's really a matter of a couple of weeks to
pick it up again. I wanted to study in France,
and it took me two years to learn French to the
level that allowed me to be admitted to one of
the top state universities. That being said,
nothing is impossible for me ;) Je pourrai
faire la recherche, la correspondance, la tra-
duction et tout ce qu'on doit préparer en
français, pas de problème.

I'm a fiction writer, and I want this position because I'd like to be involved in the en-
tertainment industry and the creative writing
business. I know everything about self-publishing and marketing/public relations. My Master's
degree in journalism (correct, I have two) al-
lows me to conduct research in the most effec-
tive way. And finally, Jeremy, my good sense of
humor will be a major addition to our full-time
collaboration, hopefully long-term.

Please see my resume attached.

I look forward to working with you.


Best,
Mila

**From:** bqczn-6674204776@job.craigslist.org
**Date:** Tuesday, August 21, 2018 3:24 PM
**To:** c5cb8015531b35aaa93b6de77f5495f5@reply.
craigslist.org
**Subject:** Re: Assistant to A-list Hollywood
Screenwriter/Director

Dear Mila,

I would very much like us to meet. Вы тоже говорите по-русски? Я работал над фильмом в студии «Мосфильм» в течение трех лет. I am scheduling interviews for next week. If you are available, would you let me know what days/ times might work for you. If next week is not good, let's try the week after following Labor Day. And, indeed, a sense of humor goes a long way with me.

Best regards,
Jeremy

**From:** c5cb8015531b35aaa93b6de77f5495f5@reply.craigslist.org
**Sent:** Tuesday, August 21, 2018 3:47 PM
**To:** bqczn-6674204776@job.craigslist.org
**Subject:** Re: Assistant to A-list Hollywood Screenwriter/Director

Dear Jeremy,

Да, я говорю по-русски, а также мат в случае производственной необходимости ;)
Awesome! What was the movie? Maybe I know it.
Next week works for me. My schedule is flexible, so any day after 12 p.m. is good. I suggest we break the stereotype of Monday and make it a stress-free, productive day.


Best,
Mila

**From:** bqczn-6674204776@job.craigslist.org
**Date:** Tuesday, August 21, 2018 4:18 PM
**To:** c5cb8015531b35aaa93b6de77f5495f5@reply.
craigslist.org
**Subject:** Re: Assistant to A-list Hollywood
Screenwriter/Director


Dear Mila,

Monday it is. I'll do my best on the productive stress-free front but no guarantees….
Let's try for 2 pm at ████████████ Street (between █████████████████ though closer to
████████), Apt███ The phone here is
212-███-███.
Prior to meeting, you might want to take a
stroll through the Kindle Edition of *How To
Self-Publish A Book* by Barb Drozdowich, if you
feel it would be helpful for our discussion. Or
you may be way ahead of it. A lundi prochain.

Cordialement,
Jeremy

**From:** c5cb8015531b35aaa93b6de77f5495f5@reply.
craigslist.org
**Sent:** Monday, September 24, 2018 6:00 PM
**To:** bqczn-6674204776@job.craigslist.org
**Subject:** Re: Assistant to A-list Hollywood
Screenwriter/Director


Hi Jeremy,

I hope you found the assistant you were looking for.

Jeremy, I wanted to ask you: will you write a
review for my book? Just a couple of sentences
will do, just like the writer from *The New
Yorker* kindly did for me.

You will not benefit from it whatsoever, except for having a fun time reading women's fiction and seeing your name on my book's
cover. ;)

Would you?


Best,
Mila

**From:** bqczn-6674204776@job.craigslist.org
**Date:** Monday, September 24, 2018 9:02 PM
**To:** c5cb8015531b35aaa93b6de77f5495f5@reply.
craigslist.org
**Subject:** Re: Assistant to A-list Hollywood
Screenwriter/Director

Hi Mila,

I would.

Best wishes,
Jeremy

**From:** c5cb8015531b35aaa93b6de77f5495f5@reply.
craigslist.org
**Sent:** Sunday, October 7, 2018 2:10 PM
**To:** bqczn-6674204776@job.craigslist.org
**Subject:** Re: Assistant to A-list Hollywood
Screenwriter/Director


Dear Jeremy,

Please find *New Yorkers Hate Food* attached.
When should I expect your answer/review?

Best,
Mila

**From:** bqczn-6674204776@job.craigslist.org
**Sent:** Tuesday, October 9, 2018 3:30 PM
**To:** c5cb8015531b35aaa93b6de77f5495f5@reply.
craigslist.org
**Subject:** Re: Assistant to A-list Hollywood
Screenwriter/Director

I'm in a bus so my fingers may slip but here's what I can tell you from my end. I know nothing about the woman — where she works, what she feels or believes, whether she has parents or sibs, or friends to whom she's close. I'm not even sure I know her name. There is nothing that would make me care about her. And the further I get into her catalogue of men she trashes, I like her even less. She seems shallow and places absolutely no value on her vagina. It's open for all, followed by a description of how worthless the men are, when, for me anyway, she far outdoes them in every way. By the time I got to page 57, I could not care less what happened to her. Sorry, but that's why I couldn't give you a quote. I think you have some talent as a writer, but you need some courses about what a novel is.

**From:** c5cb8015531b35aaa93b6de77f5495f5@reply.
craigslist.org
**Sent:** Tuesday, October 9, 2018 8:17 PM
**To:** bqczn-6674204776@job.craigslist.org
**Subject:** Re: Assistant to A-list Hollywood
Screenwriter/Director


Alright, that's an opinion.
Despite all that, how's the language? Easy to
read?

Best,
Mila

**From:** bqczn-6674204776@job.craigslist.org
**Date:** Wednesday, October 10, 2018 1:29 PM
**To:** c5cb8015531b35aaa93b6de77f5495f5@reply.
craigslist.org
**Subject:** Re: Assistant to A-list Hollywood
Screenwriter/Director

It's hard to know how to answer that. If you mean, is it an easy read, yes and no. You have a facility with language, but what you're writing isn't very interesting and highly repetitive, so that makes it a hard read. You lose interest pretty quickly and then you're slogging through one jerk after another. It makes no difference how fluid you are with the language if what you're writing isn't of interest. It's not a good question, I think. But I don't think I should comment any longer. You should get some other opinions, but not from friends and family, and not from internet readers who only want to say nice things so you'll keep paying them. Join a writers group.

Sent from my iPhone

Thanks but not a good fit.

I'm starting to prefer these types of rejections over AI-generated ones. At least these are genuine: a human rejected me, not a soulless algorithm created by a guy who has a problem expressing his emotions.

For information on what makes a good candidate, we would advise that you visit our website before submitting an application. The careers page will provide you with helpful information if you are thinking about working with us.

This is an automatically generated email; please do not reply to this message.

If you have an enquiry, the quickest way to get in touch is as follows:

- Log in to your account
- Click on the relevant application under Your Applications
- Scroll down to the bottom and type your enquiry in the Correspondence section
- Click Add to send your enquiry to
- Your enquiry is sent directly to your Hiring Manager

We appreciate that you are eager to receive feedback on your application and can assure you that we will be back in touch as soon as possible.

Elevator buttons should be able to be unpressed. Science already knows the technology.

Dear Ms. Mila

Here is my activist outreach to the international community: Every war begins with a lie. Let us find a way to stop the lies, to end the wars! We want to inspire you with a solution for an honest humanity by challenging the main source of injustice: Worldwide Media hypocrisy! We want to challenge the international hypocrites with the help of their weakest point: Public Opinion!

Here you find my 7 min speech https://youtu.be/FtVVZKTYzKM and 4 min teaser https://youtu.be/FtVJmt.

We are convinced we need the power of mainstream media to bring truth to the world.

Our independent free media in resistance is not strong enough to influence a lasting change. This is why we work on challenging the European public broadcasters that are collectively paid by the citizens. As we pay these media corporations, we demand their independent political view to create worldwide peace and understanding. Let us work on a media strategy to work together on that epic vision to end global hypocrisy forever.

I'm thirsty. Where's my tap water — New York's finest.

# 101

We have received your application. If you have followed our guidelines we will review it.

"I feel horrible, like a complete piece of crap, after what I said. I cannot be more embarrassed and ashamed of myself right now. I understand more than you can imagine. I don't know what the hell I was thinking. That reply reflects everything that is wrong with our society and the in-sensibility we are experiencing, as we talk so detachedly from our privileged bubble, forgetting that there are real people on the other side of the screen. Again, I'm so, so sorry!"

That's the kind of response I want at this point.

Please be aware that as your application has not been accepted, we are not associated with the activity relating to your candidacy proposal and do not endorse this activity in any way. If you choose to proceed, then this will be of your own volition and at your own risk. We will not monitor, measure or verify this activity.

Texted a friend suggesting we hang out tonight. She replied, "Working late. Such a drag." I now think of work philosophically: it may or may not exist.

How do philosophers get paid? Writing books? Please. That's like trying to make a living off selling ice in Antarctica. Nobody reads articles unless Taylor Swift's name pops up in the headline. And group gatherings? Forget about it — those require a membership fee that makes joining a country club look like a small donation.

Thank you for your application. It has been received, and we look forward to reading your resume.

We need philosophers as the last hope for revised ideals — moral and ethical benchmarks that won't have us spinning like a top on the whims of TikTok trends. Current politically shaped doctrines are working only for the consumption society, as if the next shiny object is our real purpose in life. Do you see what's happening? Revolutionary moods start forming up when someone is bored. Let's keep me busy before I start throwing my remote at the TV in protest.

We are experiencing irregularities with our email system. If you think that you missed an email from us, you are very likely right! Please resubmit your resume again.

This is an automatically generated email and it is not monitored.

I would rather be able to talk to pets instead of read people's minds. I already know what people think. They don't — they scroll.

Dear Candidate,

Thank you for taking the time to interview with us. We truly appreciate your interest in joining our team and the effort you put into the application process.

After careful consideration, we regret to inform you that we have decided to move forward with another candidate whose qualifications more closely align with our current needs. Please know this decision was not easy, as we were impressed by your experience and skills.

We will keep your resume on file for future opportunities that may better fit your profile, and we encourage you to apply for future openings.

Thank you again for your time and interest. We wish you all the best in your career and future endeavors.

Best regards,
Hiring Manager

Curiosity is better than arrogance. So I'm just curious: why never me?

Dear Mila,
We appreciate the time and effort you invested in the application process. After careful
consideration, we have chosen to move forward
with another candidate.

I don't help my plants with grow food, vitamins, or extra sunlight. They've gotta be New York tough.

# 107

Thank you for your interest in the Position at Company. After careful consideration, we have chosen to move forward with another candidate. We appreciate the time and effort you invested in the application process, and we encourage you to apply for future opportunities that may better match your skills.

Sincerely,
Management

I never read reviews of movies and shows I want to watch. The reviews might be great, but some people also can't find most countries on the map. The majority doesn't necessarily mean right.

Thank you for your interest in the position and for taking the time to apply. After careful consideration, we regret to inform you that we have decided to move forward with other candidates whose qualifications more closely align with our current needs.

The easiest way to keep top secrets is not in a bunker with locks, guards, and multiple levels of access. Just put all top secrets in a self-published book on Amazon, and no one will ever find out.

# 109

Dear Mila,

Thank you for applying. After careful consideration, we have decided to move forward with another candidate.

We appreciate your interest in our company and wish you the best in your future endeavors.

Construction noise makes one feel alive, and not by evoking the promise of a bright future in a newly built establishment; instead, it stirs a feeling of raw rage. And it's still not the worst: big city life can prune your ability to feel, and rage is nonetheless a very strong feeling, available just around the corner at your earliest convenience.

We appreciate your interest and the time you took to apply for the position. After reviewing your application, we've decided to proceed with another candidate. Please feel free to apply for future openings, and we wish you success in your job search.

I need change. I want to do something new — significantly new, more than just getting a short bob.

# 111

Dear Hiring Manager,

I hope this message finds you well. Thank you very much for offering me the position at your company. After careful consideration, I have decided to decline the offer.

This was not an easy decision, as I was very impressed with the Company and the people I met during the interview process. However, after weighing my options, I believe this is the best choice for my career at this time.

I sincerely appreciate the opportunity and your time throughout the recruitment process. I wish the company continued success, and I hope our paths may cross in the future.

Warm regards,

Mila

We appreciate the time you spent applying with us. After a thorough review, we've decided to proceed with another candidate. However, we encourage you to apply for future roles that may align with your skills.

Thank you again for your interest, and best of luck with your job search.

Kind regards,

Hiring Manager

You'd think job boards would want to help people find jobs without charging them upfront. Yeah, right. Job board websites want me to pay to increase my chances of being paid attention to and then pay more to have a slight chance of getting paid, sometime later, but no guarantees.

# 113

After careful consideration, we have chosen to move forward with another candidate.

We appreciate the time and effort you invested in the application process, and we encourage you to apply for future opportunities that may better match your skills.

Best regards.

I miss corruption.

# 114

Dear Mila,

Unfortunately, your professional experience does not meet our particular need at this time, but thank you for giving us the chance to review your portfolio.

Good luck in future.

I'm not looking for work — I'm data mining.

# 115

Thank you for your enthusiasm to apply to our agency. With much consideration, we have decided to focus on promoting our current employees.

Okay, who do I pay? Take my money to give me yours.

Dear Ms. Ilkova,

Thank you for your email. I am sorry I don't have better news.

Unfortunately, we will not have any new vacancies for the foreseeable future.

Selling a brain.
Year of production: 1985.
In perfect condition with upgraded features. All-season climate control, "better not touch that" sensors, auto-mode "funny," mood stabilization system after a good meal, leather interior, regular maintenance only at authorized dealers. Service book with all records available. First and only owner. Willing to trade for a good man, preferably also without a brain, so we can make beautiful children.

Dear Ms. Ilkova,

Thank you for your query and for your interest in our agency. Upon review, unfortunately we don't feel this project is right for us, so we will not be making an offer of representation. You have our very best wishes for the success of this book and of your writing career.

Sincerely,
Gretchen van Nuys
Assistant to Stephanie Tade

Did I send my resume to a book agent, or did they dare to reply to my query a year later? Some people act like they have a spare life.

## 118

Automatic reply: I'm at an offsite today and not on email until the morning of Tuesday. Thank you for your patience.

Most of our feelings were formed by movies. Glass of red wine near the fireplace, standing alone staring far away, the rain-soaked kiss preferably at the airport, the battle, where everything seems lost until you suddenly find inner strength and turn into a go-getter monster. You feel that? Then you turn around, and while the world fades away and the inspirational music gets louder in the background, you whisper to yourself: I am okay.

# 119

Thank you for your application, we appreciate your interest in joining us.

I am pleased to confirm that we have received your CV and you will be considered. We'll be having a good look through your application as soon as we can and determine if this role is the right fit for you.

In the meantime, keep updated with our latest vacancies and the exciting things we get up to on our <u>LinkedIn page.</u>

Thank you again for your time and effort and we wish you the best of luck with your application.

Talent Team

This would be the perfect time, like in Hollywood movies, when I give a speech and people, overwhelmed with empathy, give me what I want.

Dear Mila,

Thank you for your interest. After reviewing your qualifications, we have selected another candidate for the position.

We appreciate your time and wish you success in your future endeavors.

Of course it didn't work out. Either Hollywood has to make realistic movies or people in real life have to act like in Hollywood movies. Seriously, everybody, sync!

# 121

Dear Mila,

Thank you for applying. While we were impressed by your skills and experience, we have decided to pursue a candidate whose qualifications more closely align with the role.

We encourage you to stay connected and apply for any future openings that may be a better match. Wishing you the best in your job search and career journey.

Warm regards,

Hiring Department

The real workers are outside the factory.
The real leaders are outside the big politics.
The real information is outside the mass media.
How do you see the world?

Dear Mila,

We appreciate the time and effort you invested in the interview process. Your interest in
our company means a lot. After careful consideration, we have chosen to move forward with
another candidate, who was more determined to
get the role.

Best regards,
Hiring Team

More determined? I sent
you 6 follow-up emails.

Dear Mila,

Thank you for your application. After reviewing all candidates, we have decided to proceed with someone else for this position.

We were impressed by your qualifications and would love to stay in touch. We hope you'll consider applying again in the future as new opportunities arise.

Sincerely,
Hiring Manager

When someone on the internet tells you they are about to reveal a secret of some sort, they often don't know anything, not even basic things.

# 124

MAILER-DAEMON@mail159c38.carrierzone.com
Returned mail: see transcript for details
The original message was received from
mail-40137.protonmail.ch [185.70.40.137]

----The address had permanent fatal errors---
----Transcript of session follows----
552 5.2.2 User's mailbox is full

I saw a short, overweight female firefighter. I'm sure she's got some serious fire-fighting prowess. But please, God, save us all, just in case.

Thank you for taking the time to apply and interview at our company.

After evaluating all candidates, we have made the difficult decision to move forward with another applicant whose experience more closely fits our current needs.

We greatly appreciate the opportunity to learn more about your skills and experience, and we encourage you to apply for other roles with us in the future.

People who use the phrase "good vibes only" have the worst vibes.

Dear Mila,
We truly enjoyed learning more about you and
your experience through your application for
the position. Although we've decided to move
forward with another candidate, it's clear that
you have a lot to offer.

Thank you for considering us, and we hope you
find a great opportunity that aligns with your
goals. Please keep us in mind for future opportunities.

Kind regards,
Hiring Manager

When I was receiving rejection
letters from book agents, some
of them died along the way. Do
you see what I'm getting at?

# 121

After careful consideration, we have chosen to move forward with another candidate.
We wish you success in your job.

Feeling like a ROCKSTAR today, and nothing can change that. I said nothing, nothing, NO-O-O-thi-i-i-i-i-i-i-i-NG (with Whitney Houston voice).

Thanks so much for applying with our company and for your interest. After reviewing all applicants, we've decided to move forward with another candidate who's a better fit for our current needs.

Please feel free to apply again in the future. We look forward to hearing from you and we wish you all the best in your career!

This is a totally optional self-identification, but you're required to complete it even if you do not wish to answer. Rest assured it will not affect your application, but do know that we also have a quota for specific demographics, and that is not optional at all.

Thank you for applying. We were impressed by your background but have decided to go in a different direction for this role.

We encourage you to stay in touch, as there may be future opportunities that are a great fit for your skills and experience.

Best of luck with your search.

Which one is it? Still a no? At least some sort of stability in life.

Thank you for your message.

To people who think they'd be too bored to live forever had they the opportunity...

There are so many books to read, movies to watch, walks to take, adventures to make, strangers to meet, friends to greet, meals to try, songs to cry to, places to explore, stories to tell, stories to listen to, sunsets to see, dreams to chase, memories to create, love to spread, laughs to share...

# 131

Dear Mila,

Thank you for considering us. After careful evaluation, we have selected another candidate for the position.

We were impressed by your qualifications and appreciate the time you spent throughout the interview process.

We wish you all the best in your future endeavors and hope you find the right opportunity soon.

Sincerely,
Management

How many rejections did famous people get before they were hired? Hm... Not all of them started their own businesses, but many did pursue entrepreneurial ventures and took control of their careers in unique ways. A unique way might be the only way. Got it.

Dear Mila,

Thank you for taking the time to meet with us and share your qualifications. We truly enjoyed learning more about your background, skills, and experiences. After thorough discussions with the hiring team, we have made the difficult decision to pursue a candidate whose experience and skill set more closely align with our current needs.

Please know this decision does not reflect a lack of appreciation for your accomplishments or potential. We were impressed by your qualifications, and we hope you will keep us in mind for future opportunities. We wish you all the best in your continued professional journey and encourage you to stay connected.

Thank you again for your time and effort throughout the process.

Warm regards,

Karen

A sad face can be in two cases: something happened and nothing happened.

Dear Mila,

First and foremost, thank you for your time and interest. It was a pleasure to learn about your professional achievements and the unique value you could bring. After extensive deliberation and comparing the strengths of all the candidates, we have decided to move forward with someone whose skills are more aligned with the specific challenges we are currently addressing.

We truly admire the depth of your experience and the perspective you shared during our conversations. Although we are unable to offer you a role at this time, we hope you continue to follow our organization, as we believe there could be future opportunities that are a better fit.

Thank you again for your engagement, and we wish you success in your future endeavors.

I don't know why using humor as a self-defense mechanism is considered inappropriate: if you laugh at problems, they disappear.

# 134

Hello! I apologize for the inconvenience.

My name is Alice. We can offer you a part-time or full-time online job to help us with our online work. You can work from home, with flexible hours, and only need to invest 10-20 minutes per day. This will not interfere with any other work you may be doing. You can earn $150 to $1200 per day, and get paid immediately when the work is completed each day.

Are you interested?
Contact me via WhatsApp: +14049526080

Ads, recommendations, subscriptions, unhelpful sites with more pictures than words, services split up between 300 platforms, content written by robots for robots, links, links, links, good content exclusively available for a yearly fee and guarded by paywalls, and all I was looking for on the internet is: Do ants ever get lost?

Thank you for your interest. We are currently not hiring, please check our social media for exact date when we will.

Thanks again for your interest,
Team

There are no decent watches for women that are mechanical, auto-matic self-winding, waterproof, shock-resistant, stainless steel, fully luminous, with sapphire glass and an alarm, have a beautiful design, and don't cost $30,000, while women need it the most because their clock is ticking. Unfair.

Dear Mila,

We greatly appreciate the time and energy you invested in the interview process. It was a pleasure learning about your background and your approach to problem-solving. After careful evaluation of all candidates, we have made the decision to move forward with someone else whose qualifications align more closely with the current objectives of the role.

That said, we were highly impressed by your skill set and professionalism. While we are not able to extend an offer at this time, we want to express our genuine appreciation for your interest. Thank you once again for your time, and best of luck in your continued job search.

Imagine this: everyone in the street is walking with their heads down and instead of a phone, it's books. They are bumping into trees, cars, and each other because the story got too exciting and they can't stop reading. Would you get angry at those people?

Dear Mila,

It was a pleasure meeting with you and getting to know more about your background and expertise. After careful consideration, we have decided to pursue a candidate whose experience aligns more closely with the role's specific requirements.

We were very impressed by the knowledge and enthusiasm you brought to the process, and we hope this decision will not deter you from considering future opportunities with us. We are confident that your skills will be highly valuable to the right team, and we sincerely wish you the best of luck as you continue your career search.

Please feel free to stay in touch and check back with us for other roles that might be a better fit for your talents in the future.

Warmest regards.

I tried AI to write something in my style. It can never take over my job :)

Thank you for your email. This message confirms the receipt of your email.

Happiness is to enjoy. It doesn't matter what you enjoy: work, a long walk, entering an air-conditioned room on a hot day, texting with a friend, the smell of coffee, reading a book, reading random writing on the wall of a public bathroom, the yawning of a cat, a new pair of shoes you bought in summer and can't wait for autumn to start, carrot cake, the smell of the ocean, walking on the grass barefoot, finally peeing when you wanted to for a long time, watching a snow day from the inside, chocolate, seeds you didn't care about growing into a giant grapefruit, having something to look forward to.

Mila, we want to emphasize how much we appreciated learning about your unique perspectives. It's clear you have a bright future ahead of you. While we can't offer a position at this time, we wish you nothing but success and fulfillment.

A surprising link between video gaming and surgical skills has emerged from a study conducted: "Young surgeons who previously played video games for at least 3 hours a week made 37% fewer errors, were 27% faster, and scored 42% better overall than those who never played video games."

My research reveals that young surgeons who previously studied and practiced for at least 3 hours a day made 90% fewer errors overall. The video game and medical industries paid no $$ for this promotion, although they should have.

Dear Mila,

Thank you for taking the time to meet with us and for your interest. After careful review of your qualifications and conversations with our team, we have decided to move forward with another candidate who we believe better fits the immediate demands of the role.

tart tärt NOUN
— A pastry shell with shallow sides, no top crust, and any of various fillings.
— A woman considered to be sexually promiscuous.

A pie AND a slut? It's like English decided to throw a tea party at a strip club. I love this language.

# 141

Dear Mila,

Thank you so much for taking the time to apply and interview with us. We thoroughly enjoyed getting to know you and hearing about your experiences. After much discussion and review, we have decided to move forward with another candidate who is a closer match for the immediate needs of the role.

We want you to know that we were impressed with your qualifications and the thoughtfulness of your approach.

We truly wish you the best in your career and hope our paths cross again.

Best wishes,
Hiring Team

The funniest person in the room is the smartest person in the room. Only smart people have a great sense of humor.

Thank you for your time and interest in the role. We sincerely enjoyed the opportunity to get to know you and learn about your impressive background. After thoughtful consideration, we have chosen to move forward with a candidate whose qualifications better align with the current needs of the team.

Thank you again for your effort and time. We wish you all the best in your future endeavors.

Gray hair is just a lack of contrast in color, like in a photo editor.

# 143

Hi Mila,

We want you to know that your application was given serious consideration, and we are grateful for the chance to learn more about you. Even though we offered the position to another candidate, we hope you will continue to stay in touch.

I just need simple female pleasures to enjoy life to the fullest: Rent out a few apartments in NYC and be called Madam Owner.

Dear Candidate,

Thank you for your time and effort throughout the interview process. It was a pleasure to learn more about your career journey and the unique value you offer.

Your qualifications and experience were truly impressive, but we have decided to proceed with a different candidate for the role.

Shower thought number 26488: Will a gypsy steal horses while playing chess?

Hi, Mila,

Thank you for sending this along. I read your letter with interest, but I'm afraid I'm going to pass.
I do wish you every success!

Regards,
Founder & CEO

Unlike physics, economics is a subjective science. If something goes downhill and too many people suffer from it, just cancel some approaches, big deal.

Thank you for your time and consideration.

While this role wasn't the right fit at this time, we hope you will stay in touch. There may be future opportunities that align more closely with your skills, and we would welcome the chance to connect again.

Best of luck as you continue your job search.

After careful consideration, thoughtful reflection, and having weighed out all the facts, I came to the conclusion that Mom is right about everything.

# 141

Hi Mila,

Thank you for sharing your portfolio with us.

This automatically generated email is confirmation of its arrival. If we feel we can discuss it further, we will email or call you directly. If not, we won't respond further.

As we can't respond personally to everyone, please don't interpret a lack of response as a judgment.

Keep Trying!

I wish I could change the world...
Oh, no, not like that. Okay, maybe like that but definitely not alone. I was just singing Eric Clapton's song. Ugh, now I kinda want to change the world. Why did you mention it?

Thank you for your message and thank you for taking the time to apply with us.

We were impressed by your qualifications and the insights and we value your expertise. After thoughtful review, we have made the decision to move forward with another candidate who more closely fits the needs of the role at this time.

While we cannot offer you a position right now, we encourage you to stay in touch and consider future opportunities.

*Without culture, everything's in vain.*

Thank you for taking the time to interview with us.

We were impressed by your qualifications and the insights you brought to the conversation. After thoughtful review, we have made the decision to move forward with another candidate who more closely fits the needs of the role at this time.

While we cannot offer you a position right now, we encourage you to stay in touch and consider future opportunities.

Tinder profile:
"I have a lot of low lighting and 4 pillows on the bed because I'm a pretty, pretty princess."

Dude, just a heads up: 2 princesses can't fit on 1 bed.

Dear Mila,

Thank you so much for your interest.
We are sorry to tell you that we have decided
to pass.

We wish you the best of luck.

Thank you. I mean it. I wish me so much
luck that I can barely carry it home,
like I typically carry grocery bags
while cursing that poor chicken that's
already dead.

Dear Candidate,

It was a pleasure meeting with you and learning about your impressive qualifications. We sincerely appreciate the time and effort you put into the interview process. After careful consideration, we have decided to pursue another candidate whose experience better aligns with the current requirements of the role.

That being said, we truly appreciated your professionalism and the thoughtful approach you brought to our discussions. While we are unable to offer you a role at this time, we hope to stay in contact as future opportunities may arise that are a better fit for your background.

Thank you again for your time and interest. We wish you success in your job search and hope to connect again in the future.

Any rejection letter is like Schrodinger's cat: until the letter is opened, it is both a rejection and a proposal.

Dear Mila,
Thank you for your time and effort throughout the interview process. Unfortunately, we've decided to go with another candidate... in this dimension. In another parallel universe, we're sure you'd be a perfect fit. Unfortunately, in this reality, we found someone else.

Message: "Hello, are you looking for a job? I'm Lucie from EMOTE, we have remote positions available, work can be done from home, 30-60 minutes per day, you can earn from $100-500 a day, pay is paid the same day, can I share more information here?"

Ah yes, Lucie, just what I've been waiting for! Go ahead and send me your PayPal, social security number, your mother's maiden name, and don't forget a couple of iTunes gift cards — you know, for verification purposes.

# 153

Dear Mila,

First, we want to thank you for applying. It seems there's been a mix-up! After reviewing your application, we realized you applied for a role in our organization, but unfortunately, we're looking for someone with... different intergalactic experience.

Found out about Bhutan, full of phallus paintings on every house there, meant to bring good luck and prosperity for the household. The happiest place on Earth exists. Fairy tale city, dream city; you fall into its grasp and disappear forever. I'm moving.

Dearest Mila,

Verily, thou art a worthy candidate, yet alas, the stars did not align in thy favor. Though thy skills did shine brightly as the moon on a clear summer's eve, we have chosen to pursue another for the role.

Take heart, noble applicant, for the winds of fate may yet bring us together anon. In the meantime, we bid thee good fortune on thy quest for employment.

Yours in perpetuity,
The Shakespearean Hiring Manager

I don't understand why evolution is being slow with human beings who lie. There should be some sort of indication, like a giant black hair immediately sticking out of their ear, Pinocchio style.

Dear Mila,

Your application for the role has been... reviewed. Mwahahaha! While you've demonstrated incredible skills, unfortunately, you lack the necessary experience in world domination and secret lairs. We need someone who's already constructed a doomsday device, and, sadly, your resume was light in that area.

Do not despair, mortal. Your potential is immense, but we must move forward with someone who is already plotting to take over the universe. Good luck, and may we meet again on opposing sides of global conquest.

Best villainous regards,

The Supervillain Hiring Manager

Humanism always goes after order; otherwise, it causes anarchy.

Dear Mila,

It's not you. It's us. No, really! You're amazing - you have all the right skills, the perfect qualifications, and honestly, we're sure you'll make someone else very happy. But we've decided to see other candidates. We just need some space to explore other options.

Please understand that this doesn't mean we don't value you. We hope we can still be friends and that maybe someday in the future, we'll reconnect. But for now, it's over.

Wishing you nothing but happiness,
The Breaking Up with You Hiring Manager

You're just walking down the street, aimlessly, for the fun of it, and then suddenly you smell your childhood friend's living room when you both went upstairs to her apartment because her grandmother didn't want to throw down candy from the 3rd floor of a 5-story walkup.

# 157

Brave Mila,

You have embarked upon a valiant quest in search of the fabled employment opportunity. You battled through the interview gauntlet with honor and skill. However, the great Oracle has spoken, and it appears another warrior has claimed the prize.

Fear not, for your journey does not end here. The land is vast, and many other opportunities await you. May fortune guide you on your path, and may your sword remain ever sharp.

With respect,

The Fantasy Epic Hiring Manager, Keeper of the Resumes

What excites me about coming to work is getting paid. I like it a lot. Where I see myself in 5 years is getting paid significantly more.

Hear ye, hear ye, Mila!

By royal decree, after careful review by the high council of hiring lords, it hath been decided that another shall be chosen for the role thou seekest. Thy skills are indeed noble, yet another contender hath emerged with more prowess in the ancient art of spreadsheet sorcery.

We bid thee good fortune and trust that thou shalt find a kingdom more fitting for thy talents.

By the king's hand,
The Royal Decree Hiring Manager

Some people in the city seem dead inside, so technically there are walking and breathing corpses all over. But hey, who needs a pulse in NYC when rats run in front of you and scare you to death anyway?

Ladies and gentlemen, what a game we had here! Mila came in strong with her resume in the first quarter, showing off some solid skills. But as we hit halftime, another candidate stepped up with an incredible pivot — the crowd was on their feet!

Unfortunately, in the final minutes, Mila couldn't quite clinch the victory. The other candidate sealed the deal with a last-minute interview answer that was nothing short of spectacular.

But what a performance! We're sure Mila will land a touchdown elsewhere soon!

Until next season,
The Sports Announcer Hiring Manager

New PR idea on the road to fame: become a regular at a cafe or an open mic so people recognize you. Going to the supermarket every week doesn't do much.

Oh Mila,
Your skills shine like morning sun,
But no job for you.

It's not meant to be,
Another path calls your name,
Best wishes, farewell.

Sincerely,
The Haiku Hiring Manager

Ad features a bra,
Hiring — apply, they say.
What bust do they want?

Big or small,
Charm won't seal the deal.
The fit is key.

# 161

Mila,

After much deliberation, we regret to inform you that you have not been selected to move forward in this process. While you have survived the challenge rounds with grace and skill, the final tribal council has spoken, and you will not be the one to receive the metaphorical rose (or job offer).

Please pack your knives, and don't forget to check the exit interview on your way out. You've been chopped.

Best of luck in your next challenge,
The Reality Show Hiring Manager

Why do some men who are emotionally available, financially stable, ready to settle down and raise kids have looks that scream "I just had a fight with a lawnmower" — and it won?

Dear Mila,

We were deeply moved by your application, but unfortunately, due to the impending apocalypse, we have decided to place our hiring process on hold. While your qualifications are exceptional, we are now more focused on building underground bunkers and gathering supplies.

Should society rebuild, we encourage you to reapply. In the meantime, we wish you the best of luck navigating the end of days.

Doomed but sincerely,

The End of the World Hiring Manager

Kids are being lied to about Santa, grown-ups are being lied to about democracy, but don't worry, it all works out: everybody dies in the end anyway.

# 163

Hey Mila,

We just wanted to drop a quick note and let you know we've decided to go in a different direction for this role. Your skills were, like, really cool, but we're looking for someone with a bit more... artisanal experience, you know? Someone who can handle spreadsheets but with, like, a sustainable vibe.

Feel free to swing by our space sometime and grab a fair-trade coffee. We're sure you'll find your niche somewhere soon. Keep it organic!

Cheers,
The Hipster Hiring Manager

News headline: "Revolution in public peeing! NYC now has public restrooms installed throughout the city."

As someone who lived through 2 revolutions, this one is merely a public necessity. If they start shooting and burning tires demanding more pee, then it's a revolution.

Dear agent,

Your mission, was to infiltrate our organization and secure the coveted role. After a thorough review of your dossier, we regret to inform you that another operative has been selected for this mission. While your qualifications were impressive, the agency requires someone with more specialized espionage skills.

This email will be destroyed after reading, leave no trace of your previous application.

Stay undercover,
The Spy Hiring Manager

Top secret telegram  — — — — . — — . — — . . . . — . —
. . — . . — — . . — — . . . . — — . . — . . — — —

They joined forces, formed the 'Free Pee Coalition,' drafted Bill 276 with the NYC Council, and demand accessible bathrooms in all public buildings. No plan to storm the White House yet, though who knows what that holding—on—to—their—pee demographic is capable of. If anyone asks — I'm pro-choice, pro-pee, profound. Waiting for further instructions.

Dear Mila,

After careful consideration of your application, we've decided to go with someone who is slightly less perfect than you. Honestly, it feels weird to turn you down, but we didn't want you to have everything in life. A small obstacle, such as this, might help you build character and appreciate the next opportunity more. We hope you understand. We were just trying to look out for you.

Sincerely,

The Reality Check Hiring Manager

What was put up on a shelf as majorly important, something incredibly hard to kick out of your mind, whatever made you overthink and even suffer, then one day suddenly evaporates and becomes just as significant as the wind gusts forecast. Nothing provoked the change. You woke up in the morning, the usual: had a cup of coffee, pooped, and a genius idea hit you right on the toilet (where else if not there?): You're free.

Greetings, Earthling!
We have reviewed your credentials from our intergalactic headquarters, and while your qualifications are impressive by human standards, we require someone with superior extraterrestrial abilities. Your lack of knowledge in galactic diplomacy and space station engineering was ultimately your downfall.

Don't be disheartened — alien invasion is just around the corner, and we're sure there's a galaxy out there where your skills are truly valued.

Should your species evolve, we encourage you to reapply. Until then, keep your space clean.
Yours interstellarly,
Best cosmic regards,
The Alien Hiring Manager

Why can't I travel anywhere I want in the world like in the 18th century when you could just go without bothering with visas and all the bureaucratic nonsense? But no, you need a PhD in paperwork just to visit a new country on planet Earth that's for everybody.

Dear Mila,
After an extremely thorough evaluation of your application, I regret to inform you that we will not be moving forward with you for this role. The chosen candidate embodies everything that is required for success: the level of precision, discipline, order, absolute focus and is a meticulous nudnik.
Best regards,
The Typical German Hiring Manager

After Germany abandoned cheap energy sources and the automobile industry collapsed, the country is transitioning to hobby-horsing as the best green transportation option.

Hey Mila,
Thanks a bunch for applying and sharing your vibes with us. We took a good look at your application, and while we're super impressed, we're moving forward with someone else for this role. It's nothing personal — just one of those things.
We know that every setback is just a setup for a comeback. So keep shining, stay positive, and remember that the perfect opportunity is out there waiting for you. Maybe it's just around the corner — or at the next beach bonfire!
Wishing you all the best and some sunny days ahead. Keep surfing those waves of opportunity!
Cheers,
The Typical LA Hiring Manager

Maybe I should move. But where can I go after New York? Where can I live after New York? LA? I've never wanted to live in LA. I know a lot of people who love it there, though. LA is great for the weather but doesn't really hold up to the rest. New York is a blessing and a curse. There's nothing new after New York.

Dear Mila,

Alright, let's get straight to it — thanks for applying. You put in the effort, and that counts for something. But after taking a good look, we've decided to go with someone else for this role. Simple as that. You're good?

Don't take it too hard. In this city, you learn pretty quick that not every opportunity is the right fit. You're good.

There are a million other chances out there, and I'm sure one of them is just waiting for someone like you.

So, you're good. Dust yourself off, grab a slice of pizza, and keep hustling. New York's got plenty of opportunities, and I'm sure you'll find one that's perfect for you.

Good luck out there,
The Typical New Yorker Hiring Manager

Fuck. I'm good.

Dear Mila,

First of all, grazie mille for your application! We've taken a good look at it, and I have to say, your enthusiasm was like a big, warm plate of spaghetti with my family's secret marinara sauce — delicious and full of flavor. But in this moment, we decided to move forward with a mushroom risotto.

Don't let this get you down. Enjoy a good meal, have a glass of vino, and remember: every no brings you one step closer to a vai a farti fottere.

Buona fortuna,

Ciao

The Typical Italian Hiring Manager

Mamma Mia!
Here we go again.

# 111

Dear Mila,

Thank you so much for applying and for the time and effort you put into your application. We truly appreciate your interest in joining our team. After reviewing all the candidates, we've decided to move forward with someone else for this role.

But don't worry! This isn't the end of the road. Think of this as one of those detours that just might lead you to an even better opportunity. The job market is like a big, open highway; like Frankie said, "I did it my way." I just want to live while I'm alive. It's my life.

Best of luck, and keep on trucking!

Sincerely,

The Typical American Hiring Manager

Where's the fine line between hegemon and racketeer?

Dear Mila,
Thank you for your application. After a covert review involving secret meetings and shadowy figures, we've concluded that we're moving forward with another candidate. But don't let this get you down — there's always a hidden agenda at play.

Stay vigilant and keep your eyes open. There are always opportunities lurking in the shadows, just waiting for someone with your unique perspective.

Keep questioning,
The Conspiracy Theorist Hiring Manager

I came with a bunch of my books to a local bookstore and asked a buyer if I could sell my books at their store. She told me to send her an email — to my face. I can't think of 172 more imaginary objects I want to hit the stupidity out of people.

# 173

Dear Mila,

After some tough decisions, we ended up choosing someone else for this particular opportunity.

But here's the thing: you've got something to offer, and I don't want you to lose sight of that. Keep at it, because good things come to those who keep pushing ahead. I believe in you.

Best regards,

The Positive Hiring Manager

It is important to behave in such a way that history doesn't remember you as an asshole.

We've reviewed your credentials, scrutinized your experience, and weighed your talents as one might evaluate a fine wine — or a particularly intriguing bottle of ketchup. And while you didn't quite make it to the top of our list, don't be disheartened. Sometimes, it's not about the quality of the vintage but the peculiarities of taste.

You see, in our little corner of the universe, we have our own set of criteria — much like the inexplicable need for pineapple on pizza or the fascination with reality TV. Our decision was less about your qualifications and more about the cosmic dance of randomness. Maybe our office fish had a say in the matter. We'll never know.

But take heart. Life is a vast, unpredictable stage, and this is but one scene in your grand performance. Keep your spirits high. There are other companies, other opportunities, and, dare I say, other fish in the sea.

Do we really need emails if everything is connected to your phone number anyway?

Thank you for your application. After a detailed review, we've decided to move forward with another candidate. It's not that your application was a disaster — far from it. It was actually quite impressive, like finding a diamond in a pile of... well, you get the idea.

But sometimes, decisions are made not by logic but by the whims of fate or by a particularly bad cup of coffee. Our selection process can be as unpredictable as a London weather — one moment you're enjoying sunshine, and the next, you're knee-deep in rain.

So, here's to you-may your next opportunity be as rewarding as a hot cup of coffee on a frosty morning. The world is full of chances, and there's bound to be one that fits you perfectly.

Good luck, and don't let the door hit you on the way out!

The New York Public Library sent me a newsletter: "It's Banned Books Week — join with NYPL to protect the freedom to read." I see they've discovered my books. Flattered.

You obviously sent this to the wrong address. Please remove me from your contacts.

On Tinder.
Guy: Once I wanted to start a company and call it Inner G so everyone would think about the G spot.
Mila: And a secret address so no one would find it.
Guy: But I found it. Don't tell.
Mila: Founder and CEO now has a whole new meaning.

# 111

Hello, and thank you for your message. Sorry to report but this is not a good fit, good luck!

In NYC, from October 1 to May 31, building owners must maintain indoor temperatures of at least 68°F from 6 a.m. to 10 p.m. if it's below 55°F outside, and no lower than 62°F at night. Don't get me started on why it's colder at night than in the morning — logic doesn't apply here. The real issue is 55°F outside. Once your radiator hits 68°F, the apartment turns into a sauna, and you're paying for the discomfort. After a few hotline calls and office visits, I realized 1 thing: I've got nothing left but change the laws in this country.

# 178

After an exhaustive and nearly existential review of your application, we've concluded that we're going to take a different path.

It's not that you weren't great — far from it. You see, in our organization, we don't just choose people based on resumes. Oh no, we also consider things like the alignment of the stars, the quality of our coffee, and whether or not the office dog approves. It's a delicate balance, much like choosing which lottery numbers to play.

Best of luck.

Breathable underwear, training courses to breathe with your vagina, and the world is suffocating with idiots.

# 119

Sorry, but thank you for your interest!

No Smoking
No Littering
No Spitting
No Radio Playing
No Talking On The Phone
No Talking Of Any Kind
No Eating
No Drinking
No Spitting After Eating
No Puking After Drinking
No Singing
No Dancing
No Magic Tricks
No Breathing
No Woman No Cry
And Wash Your Hands Before
Returning To Work

# 180

Don't worry — life is full of opportunities. Keep applying, stay positive, and you'll find the right fit.

And remember, "Man plans, and God laughs." So, keep planning and keep laughing.

Your perfect opportunity is out there.

All the genders in the world come into a bar and say: "A table for 2, please."

# 181

We've gone through the applications, and you were perfect for this role, but we chose some-one else.

Friendship in the United States is not emotional — it's functional.

Dear Mila,

Back in my day, we didn't have all these fancy ways of applying for jobs, but one thing's the same: hard work and persistence. You showed both of those, and it made a big impression. Unfortunately, we've had to go with someone else for this role. But listen, don't get discouraged. You've got the drive, and that's what's going to take you to the next level. You just keep at it, and I'm telling you, you'll get where you need to go.

Best of luck,
The Old-School Hiring Manager

Sometimes I feel like I'm doing some NONSENSE instead of following my dreams, but then I remember people who take hobby-horsing seriously.

# 183

Dear Mila,

I know how this feels. You put your heart and soul into this process, and that means a lot.

After careful consideration, we decided to move forward with another candidate, but I want you to know that this decision wasn't easy.

You've got something special. I've seen it. Keep showing that to the world, because your time is coming. The right opportunity is just around the corner.

Stay strong, and keep the faith.
The Empathy Hiring Manager

I still have a crush on that actor. Our kids would've been pretty. Besides, kids get intelligence from their mother so we'd score 2 out of 2. But the actor is as dumb as he is pretty. Looks fade within time. He's got like another 10 years with his pretty face and then what? He's no George Clooney. Even George Clooney is no longer George Clooney.

Dear Mila,

Greetings from the future! We've traveled through time to review your application, and while your skills are impressive, we've decided to proceed with another candidate for this position.

Don't lose hope — your time is coming. Keep adjusting your flux capacitor and polishing your time machine. We're sure there's a perfect opportunity awaiting you in a different timeline.

Best,
The Time Traveler Hiring Manager

Online Ad:
"Special Pricing!
$199 Unlimited Botox."

Unlimited... Hey ladies, it's the buffet of injections! Take what you can have.

# 185

Darling,

Thank you for submitting your application — absolutely fabulous effort! We've reviewed it like the latest trend.

And while you have sharp eyes, high standards, and a passion for perfection, you didn't quite make the cut this season. You know how it is! It's not that you're out of style — far from it! You've got something, but right now, we're going in a different direction, like on the runway.

Remember, darling, you've got plenty of time to shine.

Best of luck and kisses,
The Fashionista Hiring Manager

Shopping for anything suddenly became so exhausting. I think I have enough of stuff as is.

# 186

Dear Mila,

Thank you for applying. After reviewing your superpowers and skills, we've decided to move forward with another candidate who, frankly, has a bit more "super" in their superhero.

Don't hang up your cape just yet. There are plenty of other heroic roles out there — perhaps a sidekick position or a role in the next big superhero crossover. Keep fighting the good fight!

Stay away from spiders,
The Superhero Hiring Manager

The SUPERpower I'd like to have is the power of SUPERioR.

Ahoy,

We've set sail on the high seas of applications, and though your crew was impressive, we've decided to chart a course with another swashbuckler for this role.

But don't be discouraged — there are still plenty of treasure maps out there leading to your next big opportunity. Keep your compass handy and your sword sharp. Adventure awaits!

Fair winds,

The Pirate Hiring Manager

Rom is not my favorite drink, but who am I to argue? Fill it up!

Dear Mila,

Here's the truth: I've been where you are. I know what it's like to put yourself out there, to really go for something, and then not get the outcome you were hoping for. It's never easy. After reviewing all the applicants, we've decided to go in a different direction.

But don't let this get you down. You've got something special — just keep at it, and you're going to land something even better. I'm rooting for you.

With my best wishes,
The We've All Been There Hiring Manager

Biomass from plant and animal waste turned into oil millions of years later. I haven't cleaned my floors in about 3 weeks. So I'm thinking, if I just wait a little longer, I'll become an oilman — the scheme works. Who knew procrastination could lead to a whole new career path?

Thank you for your application. We reviewed it with the same care one might give to a family recipe — because every detail counts. After much deliberation, we've decided to move forward with another candidate for this position.

This decision isn't a reflection of your qualifications, which were quite impressive. Sometimes, everything has to fit just right. And sometimes, it just doesn't work out the way we hope.

Why does the iPhone group apps into one category, Productivity and Finance? One doesn't necessarily mean the other.

Dear Mila,

It is with the deepest regret that we inform you that your application has not been selected for this position. The decision was heart-wrenching and fraught with existential angst.

But fear not, for every dark cloud has a silver lining, and every Shakespearean tragedy has a sequel. Keep your spirits high and your resume polished. The fates may yet smile upon you!

Yours in dramatic despair,
The Overly Dramatic Hiring Manager

Noooooooooooooooooooooooo!!!!!!!!!!!!!!!!!!!

This email account is closed.

I don't understand people who would go hiking alone because it's dangerous, yet here I am, looking up trails within 2 hours of the city. I still don't understand what it's like to be an award-winning, acclaimed, and wealthy writer. Anytime I don't understand something, I get to experience it to understand it better. So... I'll be right here, waiting. Thanks.

Dear Mila,
After a dazzling review of your application, we've decided to hire someone else for this role. We're sure you'll find your star turn in another "next big thing" project soon.
With glitz and glamour,
The Hollywood Hiring Manager

I should have accepted that sexual harassment offer from the Hollywood producer in 2010. I'd be winning my second Oscar for Best Screenplay by now.

# 193

Dear Mila,

Let's not waste time with pleasantries. I've read your application — every line of it — and let me tell you straight: it's not happening. There's no sugar-coating it. This wasn't your fit.

Honestly, the world's a messy, goddamn chaotic place, full of bullshit jobs and menial tasks that eat away at your soul, bit by bit. You're a bright cunt worth way better.

Don't take it personally; life doesn't work that way, even if you want it to. You'll keep moving, won't you? Like we all do, stumbling through this absurd, crazy world, looking for meaning in all the wrong places. It's not about the job anyway; it's about life — the whole damn, unhinged experience of it. So go find something that lights a fire under you, because this wasn't it.

Good luck, or don't. Either way, you'll survive.

The Henry Miller Hiring Manager

I NOW UNDERSTAND why HENRY MILLER didn't want to work in this country.

Comrade,

The Supreme Council of Recruitment has reviewed your application. Unfortunately, while your efforts were valiant, another candidate has risen through the ranks to seize the role. We must always act in the interests of the collective, and this decision was made for the greater glory of productivity.

Take comfort, comrade, for your work is not in vain. The people will remember your contributions, and we trust you will find your place among the workforce.

With loyalty to the cause,

The Joseph Stalin Hiring Manager

I'm feeling violent. Alright, which hotline should I call to let it all out?

Dear Candidate,

We had a lot of great candidates, and you were right there — you really gave it your all. But after going through the applications, we had to make the tough call to move forward with someone else.

Now, don't get discouraged. You're good — really good. I'm confident that you're going to land something great very soon because folks like you don't stay on the sidelines for long.

You got this!

Best,

Hiring Manager

I have ZERO thoughts. Does that mean I mastered the art of meditation OR degradation?

I am out of the office today. I'll be back when I'll be back.

I can easily be a diplomat — I can talk to people I don't like, and that is one of the principles of diplomacy. I can do deep research, and there's an international market for buying and selling information. Oh my god! I am so good I should be the one hiring.

Dear Mila,

Thank you for your application and the interest you've shown in joining our team. After a comprehensive review and careful deliberation, we have decided to move forward with another candidate whose experience aligns more closely with our current needs.

Should you wish to contribute to our work or support our mission in any capacity, we welcome you to stay engaged with our initiatives and explore ways to do so.

Thank you again for your interest, and we wish you the best in your future endeavors.

Sincerely,
The Diplomacy Hiring Manager

In the spirit of diplomacy, my foreign partners, alias, and I would like to express our deep concerns. We are calling for an emergency meeting of the United Nations Security Council to discuss the unprecedented and unprovoked veto on my career in the United States of America.

Dear Mila,

It is with a heavy heart, and after much reflection, that I must inform you of our decision to pursue another path. Your application,
while commendable, has been set aside — not
through any fault of yours, but by the unfor-
giving hand of fate, which governs all things
beyond our control.

In this world, one often seeks meaning in
places where meaning is scarce. The pursuit of
work, like the pursuit of happiness, is fraught
with uncertainty. We are compelled by forces
unseen, by the desires of men and the absurdi-
ties of life, to make choices that we neither
fully understand nor control. So it is with
this decision.

You must not view this as a failure, for in
truth, what is failure but the inevitable conclusion to every human endeavor? We strive, we
fall, and in falling, we learn something of the
bitter, beautiful chaos of existence. I urge
you, in your moment of rejection, to reflect
upon the nature of ambition, of hope, and of
suffering, for it is only through suffering
that we come to know ourselves.

Take this rejection not as an end, but as the
beginning of deeper understanding. The world
will remain cruel, indifferent, and vast, but
within it lies the opportunity for profound
self-discovery.

May you find peace in the struggle,
The Fyodor Dostoevsky Hiring Manager

# 199

Mila,
Thank you for sharing your resume with us.
We've decide to go with another candidate.

If Dostoevsky lived today, he'd still be depressed — except this time, he'd be drowning in my rejection letters instead of grappling with the weight of existential despair; I can just imagine him trying to find deep meaning in "We appreciate your interest, but we've decided to go with another candidate."

Dear Mila,

l've spent my life fighting for the working folks, the ones who roll up their sleeves and give it their all, and you're one of those people. You really are. But after going through all the details, we had to go with someone else for this role.

I know it's tough — it's tough — but don't lose hope. Keep doing what you're doing, keep putting in the hard work, and I promise you, good things are coming. You're gonna make it.

Keep pushing forward,
The Middle-Class Hiring Manager

I am once again among people who know how to let you be — the best class.

Dear Mila,

I trust this note finds you in good spirits. First and foremost, allow me to express our sincere gratitude for your interest in pursuing an opportunity with us. It is always a pleasure to encounter individuals of such caliber.

After careful consideration and a series of thoughtful discussions among the relevant parties, we have arrived at the decision to proceed in a different direction. Please rest assured that this decision was not made lightly; rather, it reflects the precise alignment required for a role within our longstanding establishment — one built on tradition and selectivity.

Do not be discouraged; rather, see this as a mere detour on the path to greater prospects.

With the warmest regards,
The Old Money Hiring Manager

I hope you have 1 dream over and over and over again: communism wins. And then you wake up and it's not a dream.

Dear Candidate,

First off, thanks for your interest. I see a lot of potential in what you bring to the table. That said, after reviewing your application, I've decided to move forward with someone who aligns a bit more with our... well, let's call it our "vision."

It's nothing personal, really. It's just that, around here, we operate on a different level. We're growing really fast, and we need someone who can keep up with that pace and be the Jack of all trades. This isn't just a job; it's an opportunity to ride the wave of success.

This role just wasn't meant for you. But hey, no hard feelings — there are plenty of other opportunities out there. Just not this one.

Good luck out there. Keep hustling, and maybe we'll cross paths in the future. You never know in this world, right?

Best regards,

The New Money Hiring Manager, CEO and Founder

(Yes, that's right, I built this from the ground up)

On second thought, is it just me, OR doesn't communism sound all that bad? Equality and all, like for real?...

Ghosting has to be consistent. That is the only rule. Once you decide to ghost, stick to it. Ghosting and then replying a week later, and then ghosting again, and then asking "How have you been?" in a month — that's not acceptable and should be regulated by the state. When you finally meet the ghoster, you are entitled to punch them in the face. There! I am ready to create public policy.

The Ghosting Hiring Manager

Mila, Mila, Mila,

Look, I'm gonna be honest, we had a tremendous amount of applicants. Tremendous. You were
good, really good. But, and this is big, we
went with someone else. Maybe one of the best.

Nobody picks candidates better than us. We
wish you the best of luck.

You're gonna find something great. Probably
the best job, believe me. You'll win so much,
you'll get tired of winning.

Best regards,
The Donald Trump Hiring Manager

From 88D22: "Mila, can I ship my Official Campaign Hat to you? It would look great on you! Just give at least $47 before my end-of-month deadline."

My book "They Said It's True" with exclusive handwritten author's notes costs $48. Just give me at least $48. No trades.

Dear Mila,

Well, look — you did a heck of a job putting yourself out there. Seriously, we were impressed by what you brought to the table. Here's the thing: we've had some really strong folks, and you were absolutely one of them. It wasn't an easy choice, but we had to move forward with someone else this time. That said, l've been around long enough to know that when one door closes, another...oh, ice cream! The matter of fact is you've got the skills, you've got the heart, and you've got the drive. That next opportunity is out there waiting for you, and I have no doubt you're going to seize it. You fall down — you get up.

Stay positive, stay hopeful, and keep pushing forward.

Best regards,
The Joe Biden Hiring Manager

I should get some ice cream. Sugar makes you feel better. Amazon, bathtub of ice cream, free delivery today. No, I don't want anti-slip sneakers, anti-slip bicycle, and anti-slip beach half price. Ugh, never mind.

Dear Mila,

Let me first say this: You've shown incredible determination by putting yourself out there and applying for this role. That takes courage, and I respect that. After a thorough review, we've made the decision to move forward with another candidate.

There's nothing you can do about it and, frankly, neither can I. But what we can do together is laugh, as it is the only thing that can be unburdened by what has been.

The Kamala Harris Hiring Manager

Today I learned a new technique on how to instantly make yourself feel better and not let anything into your mind: ha haha hahaha hahahaha hahahaha haha— hahahaha hahahahahahaha hahahahahahahaha.

Dear Mila,

Thank you for your application and for demonstrating such talent. After careful consideration, we have chosen another candidate for this role.

But remember, every challenge is an opportunity for growth, and I know you have the spirit to overcome this setback.

In the meantime, l'd like to ask for a small favor. If you happen to have a few spare coins lying around, consider donating them to me, I mean us, I mean my country, I mean our country. This is a request for a gesture of goodwill, reinforcing the strength of our collective effort and, perhaps, securing a place in future considerations for my country's well-being, I mean my well-being.

That's one small donation for you, one giant mansion for my family.

With gratitude,

Thank you very much!

The Volodymyr Zelensky Hiring Manager

When someone asks you for a favor, know that it's something small.
When someone asks you for a small favor, know that it's something you don't want to do.

Dear Mila,
You're a fighter — I could see that right
from the start. You threw your hat in the ring,
and that's something to be proud of. After reviewing all the candidates, we had to make the
tough call and go with someone else.
But listen, this is just one round. You're
not done yet. Keep swinging, because I know
you've got what it takes to win this fight.
It's only a matter of time before you find your
next victory.
Take care of yourself,
The Classic Optimism Hiring Manager

I've been waiting for my immigration
case to move forward for 3 different White House administrations.
Within that time, you can fall in love,
get married, have kids, divorce,
learn how to play 3 musical instru-
ments, travel the whole world, pay
off a mortgage, start a few
wars, finish a few wars, create
revolutionary medicine, meet aliens...

# 209

Dear Mila,

I'm gonna level with you. This wasn't an easy decision. You've got talent, you've got smarts, and you've got a future as bright as a shining city on a hill. But after reviewing everything, we had to go with another candidate for this role. Don't let this slow you down. Keep moving, keep growing, and keep aiming high. I believe in you, and I know you're going to do big things.

Good luck. The world is watching.
Keep the faith,
The Bright Future Hiring Manager

... move to Mars, get married on Mars, have kids on Mars, get divorced on Mars, figure out how to eat sugar and not get fat, witness the rapid pace and severe consequences of global warming for ecosystems, wear bikinis outside in Siberia in February, adopt dinosaurs as pets, hit global freeze, and my case is still pending.

**Subject:** Unfortunately, Not Today.

Dear Applicant,

It is with the sort of reluctance one might experience when attempting to cancel a gym membership that I must inform you of our decision. It appears that the fates, those same ones who decide traffic jams and pizza delivery times, have deemed that you shall not move forward in this process.

We hope you are not too devastated, as our disappointment comes only second to your inevitable sense of relief that you won't need to navigate the treacherous waters of our ever-mounting paperwork, endless meetings about meetings, and general disillusionment that has kept this whole operation afloat.

And as we all know, in the end, rejections only build character. Or ulcers. But mostly character.

Your next gig might just be around the corner, who knows?

Until then, keep your chin up. The world is full of opportunities — some of them even pay well.

Best wishes in your next rejection.
Pretty much sincerely,
The Mila Ilkova Hiring Manager

If you want immortality, go to church.
If you want guarantees, buy a phone.
If you want pure love, get a dog.
You'll find what you seek, just not
exactly where you're looking.

Salut, everyone!

I'm a writer, and I can't go back to the office, remotely or on-site; I just can't.

I used to do journalism, but then the world went to shit. I used to do integrated communications, but now I could not care less about beauty products that make you look the same, or merchant cash advance that is actually bad for your mom-and-pop business, or restaurants that serve avocado toast like that piece of bread has a Michelin star.

I don't have a filter, at least in my thoughts, so cancel me all you want. What I do have is philosophical satire that I write and post online.

If you love it – please donate, so I can keep doing what I love the most – write books.

Donate: milailkova.com/donate
PayPal: paypal.me/milailkova
Zelle: +1 917 719 0794

Follow on the socials:
youtube.com/@writermilkova

instagram.com/writermilkova

Subscribe to newsletters: milailkova.com

Leave reviews: amzn.to/4gLxQV6

Many thanks.

# Mila Ilkova...writer

# ALL BOOKS BY THE AUTHOR

Рассказать другу

Теория мудака

Пароль: Сарафан

New Yorkers Hate Food

Ой, всё!

Ten Myriad Moves

Rejection Letters of Book Agents

They Said It's True

Rejection Letters of Future Employers

www.ingramcontent.com/pod-product-compliance
Lightning Source LLC
Chambersburg PA
CBHW062058080426
42734CB00012B/2684